MW00439737

JOURNAL

PETER PAUPER PRESS, INC.
WHITE PLAINS, NEW YORK

PETER PAUPER PRESS
Fine Books and Gifts Since 1928

OUR COMPANY

In 1928, at the age of twenty-two, Peter Beilenson began printing books on a small press in the basement of his parents' home in Larchmont, New York. Peter—and later, his wife, Edna—sought to create fine books that sold at "prices even a pauper could afford."

Today, still family owned and operated, Peter Pauper Press continues to honor our founders' legacy—and our customers' expectations—of beauty, quality, and value.

———

Cover illustration by Dot Dash Studio

Copyright © 2021
Peter Pauper Press, Inc.
202 Mamaroneck Avenue
White Plains, NY 10601 USA
All rights reserved
ISBN 978-1-4413-3598-2
Printed in China
7 6 5

Visit us at www.peterpauper.com

Dear Jen,

I'm so proud of you for taking steps in your journey of healing and I believe you'll come out of this a stronger and more confident person. Just know that I love you very much and support you through the process. Please let me know if I can do anything to help.

Love always,

Marti

Cake
To Leslie
Alice, Darling

1